LINTON IN PICTURES
A Photographic History

GARTH COLLARD
NORMAN DANN

Published by
Linton and District Historical Society
in association with

THE LINTON
NEWS

Published in 2006 by
Linton & District Historical Society
12 Crossways, Linton, Cambridge, CB1 6NQ

Author: Garth Collard

Designed, typeset and edited by Norman Dann
Proofreading: Alan Judge, Gloria Fidler, Kate France
Editorial Consultant: Sally Simmons

Printed by Piggott Black Bear, Cambridge, UK

ISBN 0-9539993-1-9

Further copies can be purchased from local shops or direct from
Garth Collard, 12 Crossways, Linton, Cambridge, CB1 6NQ
Tel: 01223 892395

Front cover: The Dog and Duck pub and the old wooden bridge in the early 1860s (see page 13).
Rear cover: Women of the Land Army at Little Linton Farm, 1916-18 (see page 100).

Contents

Linton's Story

The story of Linton is a rich and interesting one, stretching back thousands of years. While this book of photographs concentrates on the past 150 years, a considerable amount is known about earlier times.

The first substantive evidence of settlement in Linton is in the Iron Age. Coarse blackish-brown pottery, bone needles, sewn skins and leather working tools were discovered on the slopes of the chalk hills near Hadstock Road. The chalk pit excavations between 1948 and the 1960s, at what is now the industrial estate, revealed that Iron Age settlers from north-western Europe had established a huge rectangular settlement here between the sixth and first centuries BC.

The Romans settled all along the Granta valley and the villas at Hadstock and Bartlow confirm the importance of this area to the new invaders. The Hadstock villa lay close to Barham Hall near the river bridge on the bypass and fragments of painted wall plaster were discovered there during an excavation between 1846 and 1850. The villa seems to have been abandoned some time after the late fourth century AD. Cremated bones housed in glass urns inside a brick chamber were among the Roman finds discovered in the 1832 excavation of one of the four original great mounds located in Bartlow. During the construction of the warden's house at the Village College in 1936 the bodies of two women and children were unearthed and archaeologists dated these finds to the third century AD. Finally, the Roman Via Devana or Worstead Street just beyond Borley Wood demonstrates the extent of Roman control over the Linton area.

The Anglo-Saxons invaded Britain from the fourth century and there is plenty of evidence of their settlement in Linton. In 1853 an excavation took place on Linton Heath between the Roman Road and the present road to Haverhill revealing 104 Saxon skeletons in a cemetery site. Two decorated scabbards were also discovered and these provided further evidence of a sophisticated Saxon settlement in Linton. The *Codex Diplomaticus Aevi Saxonici* dated AD 725 contains the first recorded reference to Linton. Before 1066 all the lands in Linton were

Opposite. A 1905 photograph of Mrs Arthur Coxall and her children in front of her shop at the top of Church Lane (see p. 57).

Below. The 'Three Hills' Roman burial mounds near Bartlow, shown in this 1864 photograph during the construction of the Stour Valley railway which sliced through the fourth mound.

held by Eddeva (Edith) the Fair, believed to be the sister of King Harold of Wessex.

Norman England was divided into hundreds for administrative purposes and Linton was part of Chilford Hundred (chil = royal) along with eight other local villages. By the time of the Domesday Book in 1086 the Earl of Richmond, Count Alan of Brittany, owned the four settlements of around 400 people that make up our present village. Great and Little Linton manors (linton = flax farm) were two of these settlements, Great and Little Barham (bereham = an enclosure on a hill) formed the other two.

The first mention of a church in Linton was in 1163 but there must have been a church here in Saxon times. Linton came under the jurisdiction of the bishops of Lincoln until 1108, and was then transferred to the diocese of Ely. Great tithes (a 10 per cent church tax on corn) were awarded to the Benedictine Abbey of St Jacut de L'Isle at Dol in Brittany who established a small priory on the site now occupied by Linton House, opposite

Sweet Talk News. The priors acted as rectors of Linton, but after 1440 King Henry VI confiscated the French abbey lands and awarded them to Pembroke College, together with the control of Linton rectory. The bishops of Ely, however, still retained the sole right to appoint Linton vicars.

Linton became a flourishing market town in the Middle Ages yet never secured a royal charter to give it borough status. There was a market in Green Lane from 1246, when William de Say of Great Linton was awarded a charter for a market and fair. By 1281 this had moved to Market Lane.

The de Furneaux family, lords of the manor of Great and Little Barham, established a rival market at their end of the town. This soon disappeared but the fair continued to be held in the Emsons Close area until 1878.

Below. Iron age remains being excavated at Linton Village College in 2004. The body, thought to be female and not of noble birth because of the lack of grave goods, was uncovered during the building of the Granta School.

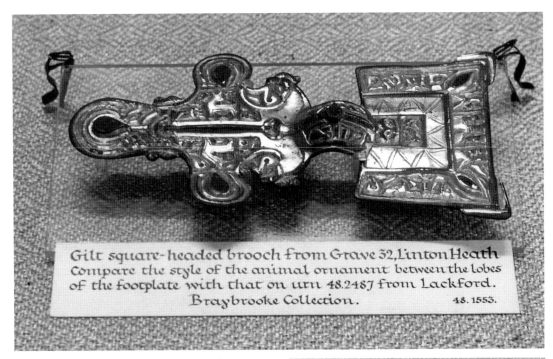

Gilt square-headed brooch from Grave 32, Linton Heath. Compare the style of the animal ornament between the lobes of the footplate with that on urn 48.2487 from Lackford. Braybrooke Collection. 48.1553.

Above and right. *Jewellery discovered during Richard Neville's excavation of the Saxon burial ground on Linton Heath in 1853, including (above) a beautiful gilt brooch now kept in the Department of Archaeology and Anthropology at Cambridge University.*

The town expanded its own trades and cottage industries but all were still dependent on the wealth generated by a thriving agricultural industry. The beautiful timber houses along the High Street and lanes which give our village its attractive appearance were largely built in Tudor and Stuart times from the money generated by these activities.

Linton market was the third most important in Cambridgeshire during the 18th century but then declined and was finally closed in 1864. The whole prosperity of the town was threatened by economic, political and social change in the first half of the 19th century. Vibrant coaching inns succumbed to the railways; leather and textile trades failed to compete with both local and northern mills; the Napoleonic wars crippled local agriculture; and the doubling of the population overstretched local housing resources. Linton ceased to be called a town once parish councils were introduced in 1894.

Prosperity temporarily returned between 1840 and 1880 when farms were enclosed to boost productivity. The malting trade based on local barley crops flourished, and the Stour valley railway line finally reached Linton in 1865. However, from the 1880s until 1939 there was a catastrophic decline in agriculture caused by the import of cheap overseas food. Linton's population fell from 2061 in 1851 to 1530 by 1901, recovering to the 1851 figure only in 1961. People moved to London or further afield and local landlords and farmers could not afford to invest in new building or repair the deteriorating cottage housing stock.

Many of the photographs in this book provide an insight into village life in this difficult economic period.

The High Street

*The High Street starts at the Greenhill, where it joins the road to Cambridge, and runs through the village to the start of Bartlow Road, near the library. The photographs in this chapter start at the Cambridge Road end and run in sequence.

The first reference to the Greenhill was in a document in Pembroke College, Cambridge, dated 1344 which mentioned 'divers cottages called the Greenhill'. The Greenhill was the high point on the south side of the Granta valley and there was a small green here until the building of the bypass in 1965.

Halfway towards the river bridge is Market Lane. This part of the High Street was the commercial hub of the village when the market moved here from Green Lane in 1281. Here were located the market stalls, the great coaching inns and the most important shops. Towards the river, the housing*

Above. Aerial view of the Greenhill around 1929 with the High Street on the right. The main road from Cambridge to Saffron Walden (top to bottom of photograph) went through the Grip before the Linton bypass was built.

Opposite. The High Street in 1918, viewed from the bottom of Balsham Road.

thins out since constant flooding made settlement near the bridge a risky proposition.

Linton Bridge was built between 1866 and 1867 and was then called New Bridge, later Swan Bridge. Before 1866 there was a ford across the river and a wooden footbridge called Westrope Bridge. Beyond the river the High Street climbs past the ancient Swan Inn towards Coles Lane and Church Lane. This part of the village was less prosperous until the mid-19th century when working class pubs and shops sprang up. The village virtually ended at the start of Balsham Road.

Above. *Linton Flower Show Triumphal Arch in 1883. The shows started in 1878 and attracted massive crowds of visitors who would have been impressed by the 'Welcome' greeting over the arch as they arrived from the station. The show was held in Eliza Ficklin's orchard, now Dr Bertram's garden, where flowers and vegetables were judged in separate classes for tradesmen and labourers.*

Below. *The top of Linton High Street in the early 1920s. William Burling's watch and clock repair business was on the right and Herbert Powell's bakery on the left. The latter became the Greenhill Café, and was finally demolished in the 1950s. Greenhill Mews occupy this site now.*

HIGH STREET FROM GREEN HILL,
LINTON, CAMBS.

Right. This view of the High Street from 1910 shows Alfred Jabez Backler on the left standing outside his butcher's shop. From the 1930s to the 1950s the Norden family owned the premises, now 25 High Street. On the right was the 'cyclery' and garage of Frederick Suckling, which from 1932 until the 1960s housed the Norden tyre business.

Below. The High Street by the old Market in the early 1890s. The old 16th-century buildings on the right, owned by the Smoothy family, were pulled down in 1900. The Literary Institute building in the centre is an 18th-century structure and was used as a club for businessmen from the 1850s until 1954. During the Second World War ration books were issued here.

High Street, Linton.

Above. *The Post Office, seen on the left in this 1910 photograph with the mail handcart outside, closed in 1920. On the right is Bull House, once the 18th-century Black Bull Inn; the iron railings were removed in 1940.*

Below. *The High Street in 1912. Chapel Terrace on the right was built around 1795 for the workmen of John Day, the builder resident at the present-day premises of Paintin's. The building with the flag was the Salvation Army Hall.*

Left. A photograph from the early 1860s of the old wooden footbridge, known as the Great Bridge of Linton from Tudor times, with the ford over the river and the Dog and Duck pub beyond. The present bridge was built in 1866–7.

Below. A mid-1920s view of Linton's main hostelry, the Swan Hotel, and one of the oil-powered street lamps first erected in 1896. On the extreme right was a German field gun given to the parish council in 1920, which fired a 15lb shell; it went for scrap in 1940.

Left. Looking towards the Swan Bridge around 1896. The two main village pumps were on the left by the trees; they were removed by 1937. The road was not tarred until 1911. The Swan Hotel was part of the Benskins chain of public houses.

Above. The former kitchen area of Linton House is on the left in this 1900 photograph. The main house was built in 1698 by John Lone, a lawyer, and before 1914 the Linton Flower Shows were held here. Coles House on the right was built in the 16th century and was named after an 18th-century corn dealer, Robert Cole.

Below. Chaundler's, on the left, was a 15th-century structure that once had a grand central hall. The cottages were used to house farm labourers from the 18th century. The Bell Inn was owned by Christmas Breweries of Haverhill and in this 1910 photograph is still covered in plaster (see page 71). On the right is Alfred Forsdike's butcher's shop.

Above. *The High Street in 1907. The little boy playing with a hoop is outside Carter's shop at no. 80. Coxall's hairdressing shop, with barber's pole, is at the end of Church Lane, and the Bell Inn is on the right.*

Below. *On the far left of this 1910 photograph are the gates of Linton Laundry, now 96 High Street, which went bankrupt in 1919. On the right is Edgar Morley's photography and newsagent's shop.*

Above. This photograph from the late 1920s shows the small Sawston-owned Linton Co-op on the right, opened in 1904, and the Waggon and Horses pub (no car park needed then!). On the left you can just see the Princess of Wales pub, demolished in 1936. Beyond it is one of Holttum's shops.

Below. An 1896 view of the High Street and the end of Balsham Road. On the right is Mr Norden's blacksmith's shop, which burned down in 1909, and the wheelwright sheds of the Rush family are on the left. The two thatched cottages are in front of an area of land which, for reasons unknown, was called Water Hall.

Medieval Violence

In August 1369 an incident took place at the junction of Bartlow and Horseheath Roads which would not seem too out of place in a 21st-century city. John Biggs of Linton was changing his horse when he was hit with a club and fell to the ground. His assailant, John Spryng of Castle Camps, then hit him again while he lay dying on the roadside. Spryng immediately fled and was never caught.

Below. *Looking towards Bartlow and Horseheath Roads in the 1920s. The cottage in the centre was demolished in 1931, and those on the right were once part of the Old Dolphin Inn dating back to the 18th century. The town crier lived here in the 1930s and organised the poster displays.*

Above. *View of Linton coming from Haverhill. The cottages on the left were recently a wool shop called Kaleidoscope. The fence marks the present-day entrance to Granta Vale; the cottages beyond were demolished in the 1950s.*

Lanes and Roads

Horn Lane

Horn(e) Lane once included the road we call Church Lane and enclosed three sides of the manorial close of the lords of Great Linton, now Dr Bertram's garden. In the photograph on the facing page, the cottages by the man on the left date from the 17th century and were the centre of Quaker activity in Linton then, but became The Chequer pub in the late 18th century. Suckling's chemist shop can be seen in the High Street.

There was a bridge recorded at the bottom of Horn Lane in 1497, and the ford was used by wagons well into the 20th century. The wooden structure acted as a barrier and accentuated flooding, but the raised causeway allowed villagers to walk to church safe from potential flood waters.

Above. Springfield House, Horn Lane, built in 1847 by John Dorrington, who also established a Classical and Commercial Boarding School on this site from 1844 to 1857 for around 30 boys aged 7 to 15.

Below. Horn Lane (or Church) bridge and ford in the 1870s.

Opposite. Horn Lane around 1912.

Cambridge Road and the Grip

Before the Linton bypass was built, the main road from Cambridge to Saffron Walden passed by the Greenhill and continued through the Grip. This was an old term for a ditch or small watercourse that sometimes dried up. The road then turned sharp right and proceeded along Hadstock Road. Water from the slopes above the present-day zoo used to run down the Hadstock Road and across the Grip meadows to the river Granta close by Horn Lane bridge.

The Cambridge Road or Lane was once quite a narrow thoroughfare, and close to the village two small lanes led off it – the Rookery, an area of squalid housing near the site of the present-day police houses, and Joiners Road.

Above. *The Greenhill pub and the Grip, taken before 1914. The cottages of Greenhill Farm, demolished around 1922, are on the left and Henry Allen's tailor's shop is by the signpost.*

Below. *Horses and hounds riding down the Grip in the 1950s. The late 16th-century cottages on the left were all owned by John Cockerton in 1600. The pavement was raised because the Grip (or Stoney Street) frequently flooded.*

Left. The Grip/Hadstock Road in 1900, looking north. The railway came to Linton in 1865 and closed in 1967 when this bridge was demolished. From the 16th century until 1783 Grip Farm on the right, which used to be much larger, was owned by the Richardson and Flack families. The barns were converted to houses in 1996.

Right. Cambridge Road in 1906. The cottage on the left is still there. The two gabled houses and the lane between them were part of the Rookery, an area of squalid housing. In 1919, 11 cottages in the Rookery were sold for a total of only £150.

Left. The Rookery in the 1930s looking towards the Cambridge Road, with Harry and Billy Hills. The cottages were built by Robert Wright in the 1830s and were known as Wright's Rookery. By 1954 they had all been pulled down; in 1958 four police houses were built on part of the site.

21

Joiners' Road, Linton, Cambs.

Above. 1931 photograph of Joiners Road

Below. The clapper stile in the 1930s with the cricket meadow and workhouse beyond.

Joiners Road

Joiners Road was named after a wealthy family of 16th-century joiners who owned most of the nearby land. The five pairs of council houses on the right were built by Paintin's between 1929 and 1931, but the land beyond the houses was used as a rubbish dump in the early 1930s. Suvla House and Essex House were the only buildings on the left-hand side before 1931.

Symonds Lane

Symonds Lane, just over Linton Bridge, was named after a 16th-century family called Simons or Seamans. Villagers later renamed it Workhouse or Union Lane after the Union Workhouse was built there in 1836 to house the poor and idle from more than 22 local villages. It was later renamed the Linton Institution, and became Linton Hospital after 1945.

The council houses in the photograph opposite were built by Mr Burgess in 1911 at a cost of

£1455. In the 1930s Symonds Lane cottages were mostly unfit for habitation and on a very cramped site. The RDC bought the last 10 cottages for £110 in 1935 and demolished them to create Hillway, where Paintin's built 18 houses and bungalows for £4580.

22

Above. *Symonds Lane cottages in the 1930s, now the Hillway site.*

Below. *Symonds Lane around 1930, with Ivy Tofts outside the first house on the right and Mr Balaam, the milkman, in the centre with his bicycle.*

Bartlow Road

Bartlow Road used to be known as Barham Road, which led to Barham Hall, the largest farm in Linton. In the photograph above, the four cottages on the left were built soon after 1840. The farm on the right, which was demolished in 1933, was run by the Fincham family between 1799 and 1857.

Above. Bartlow Road in 1905.

Below. Millicent House in Mill Lane in 1900.

Mill Lane

Mill Lane is an ancient lane leading to Hadstock (or Linton) Mill. The photograph below shows Millicent House, a 17th-century timber-framed building. An earlier house on the site was the residence of the Millicent family, lords of Barham Manor from 1420; Sir John Millicent lived here in 1607 when James I knighted him at Royston. John Adcock used the building as Linton's first post office from 1835 to 1869.

Above. *Looking down Coles Lane in 1900. On the left is the flint wall of the Manor House garden, which used to run the complete length of Coles Lane.*

Below. *Coles Lane 1900. The little girl in white is Doris Tofts.*

Coles Lane

Just up from Linton Bridge is Coles Lane, named after the 18th-century corn dealer who lived in the now beautifully restored Cole's House where our new one-way system begins.

These two photographs from 1900 show some of the 11 thatched cottages of Augustus Diddell in Coles Lane. These had all been demolished by 1936 and the occupants moved into the Hillway council houses. The area is now known as Diddell Court.

Above. Green Lane in the 1860s, one of Linton's oldest photographs.

Below. Green Lane in 1900. The chimney on the extreme left was part of the smoked fish business of Horace Morley.

Green Lane

Green Lane led to the old medieval green where Linton's first market was established in 1246. The green was walled in at the time of the enclosures in 1840. The 16th-century cottages opposite the green were mainly occupied by farm labourers and were cramped, damp and dilapidated, and almost half were demolished in the mid 1950s.

Balsham Road

The present-day Balsham Road was called Wood Lane before the Enclosures Act. A narrow lane ran to Borley Wood and the existing Balsham Road stopped near Mr Smith's scrapyard.

In 1902 there were no houses beyond the present-day entrance to Back Road, just the new terraced houses built by the Oddfellows Friendly Society around 1900, and the workshop of Mr Norden, one of four village blacksmiths.

Eight pairs of council houses were built in Balsham Road between 1927 and 1928 on Pembroke College land at a total cost of £6157.

Left. *Balsham Road in 1902.*

Below. *The new council houses in Balsham Road after 1928, and on the left, the sheds of the Perry family who were the village hurdle makers.*

Transport

Horse and Cart

Until the 1920s the main form of road transport was by horse-drawn wagons and private carriages. Apart from farm vehicles, the main horse-drawn transport on Linton's streets would have been delivery carts. Heavy goods were pulled by steam engines and accidents were fairly frequent due to overloading. Eventually regulations reduced to three the number of trailers an engine could tow.

The roads were not made up and so Linton had its own water cart to dampen the dusty streets in summer. The first tarred roads in the village came after 1911, and the contracts stipulated that a section of unmade road had to be left at the side of the tarred section for use by horses.

Opposite. Herbert Powell's horse-drawn bread delivery cart at the top of the High Street in 1900.

Above. *Herbert Morley's bakery cart in Mill Lane in the early 1920s. The man in the photograph is Jo Cottage who was a Linton postman from 1920 until 1961.*

Below. *Mr and Mrs Alfred Forsdike in their decorated pony and trap at the King George V coronation celebrations, held in the recreation ground in 1911.*

Above. Linton water cart in the 1860s pulled by a rather overworked donkey. The streets were not tarred until 1911 so water was sprinkled on the dusty road surface in the summer.

Below. A steam-hauled truck laden with sacks of grain owned by Samuel Crawley of Hadstock overturned in January 1911 at the Greenhill when the load shifted. The White Hart pub in the background was pulled down later that year.

Above right. *Mr Albert Norton of Back Road with his cart loaded up to deliver fruit and vegetables to the local villages around 1930. He grew all the vegetables on his smallholding, and his son Bill and daughter Barbara loaded the cart. The horse was also called Bill, and the net helped to keep off the flies.*

Above left. *Coote and Warren's horse-drawn coal wagon driven by Len Noakes in the early 1920s and photographed near Chaundler's in the High Street. The firm was run by Augustus Diddell and had its depot at the station.*

Below. *The largest grocery and drapery shop in Linton, with more than 2000 customers in 1918, was Holttum's on the corner of Market Lane. Mr Allen worked for them for 50 years and drove this wagon to deliver groceries and paraffin to the villages around Linton.*

Petrol Power

In 1923 Linton celebrated the arrival of the Ortona No. 13 single and double-decker buses, which provided an alternative means of transport to Cambridge and Haverhill via Abington and Linton; before then everyone travelled by train or horse-drawn wagon.

Motor vans and lorries became a more frequent sight in the late 1920s and early 1930s. Linton Haulage and Linton Light Haulage were the two main firms operating goods vehicles in the village. Holttum's grocery store was the first Linton shop to use motor vans to deliver its goods and the local ice cream manufacturer used the cheaper alternative of motorcycle and sidecar.

Top. Dr Palmer and his chauffeur around 1914 in one of Linton's first motor cars. He held his surgery at his house, Richmonds in Symonds Lane, from 1900 to 1925.

Right. Linton Haulage Company's Leyland truck parked in the Grip in the mid-1930s, with Fred Uden.

Below. The Linton & District Pure Ice Cream Company, owned by Mr Becket of Hadstock Road, made its own ice cream and ran a fleet of six motorcycles and sidecars. The rider here is Mr Andrewes of Cardinals Green.

Above left. Mr Hall at the wheel of one of Holttum's first motor vans in the 1920s. The solid-tyred Ford delivered to more than 18 local villages. The firm weighed and bagged its own sugar, tea and dried fruit.

Below. Ortona buses appeared in Linton in 1923, and this 1928 photograph was taken at the Drummer Street depot.

Above right. Albert Morley ran a wood merchant's business in the early 1950s and is pictured here with his lorry in Linton. He had previously been a fishmonger with a shop in Green Lane where the family business had operated from the 1920s to the early 1950s.

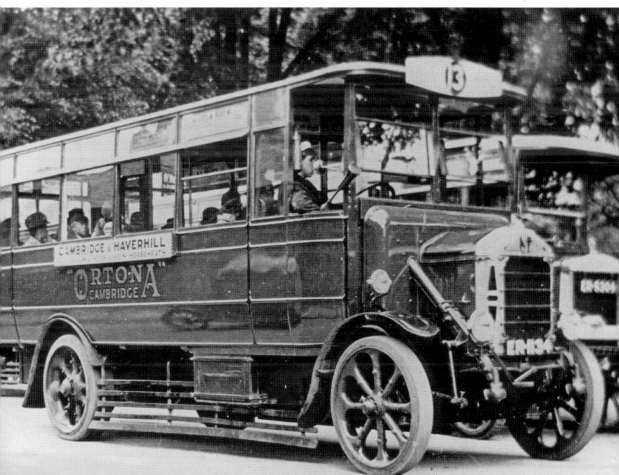

Punts and Pedals

In the 1930s the river near Hildersham was deeper than today and garden parties at the big riverside houses often provided the opportunity for punting.

The bicycle was popular from the 1890s and middle-class ladies were liberated by this new form of transport. Two bicycle sales and repair businesses were set up in the village specifically to cater for this new demand.

The Railway

The Stour Valley Railway reached Linton in 1865 and the station was the hub of trade and commerce in the village. Livestock, coal, grain and heavy goods all came via Linton station.

The Sunday schools and choirs organised annual excursions to the seaside and popular destinations were Walton-on-the-Naze, Hunstanton and Clacton. In 1909 the choir travelled to Southend to view the British fleet and eight of them went on board the dreadnought battleship *HMS Superb*.

A Special Day Out

On Thursday 7th August 1891 hundreds of Linton Church Sunday School children left Linton station at 7.45am for the two and three quarter hour journey to Clacton. This was a special trip as most had never been beyond the Bartlow Hills before. They each wore a scarlet rosette and holidaymakers were so fascinated by their appearance that crowds assembled to see them eat on the beach. Having ridden on the switch-back railway, seen a Punch and Judy show, bathed in the sea, watched a tame bear, and eaten shrimps and cake on the 1100ft-long pier they set out for home. Arriving in Linton at 11.50pm they had all enjoyed the thrill of a lifetime. The four shillings return fare (20p) paid by the Church was beyond the means of working-class parents earning 16 shillings (80p) per week.

Above left. Mona Challis and her friends from the Greenhill pub made up a punting party on the river Granta in the late 1930s near Colonel Foster's Hildersham Mill.

Left. Maude Forsdike of 74 High Street in the rear garden of her father's house around 1910. He was the local butcher.

Facing page, bottom. Late 1950s photograph of the University Railway Club train steaming by Linton station signal box. By then the regular services were pulled by diesel locomotives.

Above left. *1962 photograph of the Cambridge University Railway Club special travelling thorough Camps Cutting between Bartlow and Haverhill. The locomotive was a J15 0-6-0 number 65469.*

Above right. *Linton station around 1910. The Stour Valley line was opened on 1st June 1865 and finally closed in March 1967. The journey to Cambridge took under 25 minutes and there were four trains daily each way. A branch line to Saffron Walden and Audley End via Bartlow opened in 1866.*

Right. *Linton station platform around 1905. The passengers are probably waiting to join one of the summer excursions organised by Great Eastern Railway.*

Floods, Storms, Fire and Water

Opposite. The 1968 Linton Flood in which locals are seen cycling and walking through the floodwater near Swan Bridge.

Above. The floods in 1900 covered the recreation ground in Linton, and here local children were photographed enjoying the occasion. Stanton's Bridge is on the left and the Linton Union Workhouse on the right.

Below. A photograph from 1968 showing the extent of flooding in the churchyard.

Linton has always been subject to flooding and with a few exceptions, such as the Dog and Duck, no housing was built close to the river until the early 19th century.

Here is a selection of photos that show the effects of flooding from 1900, 1968 and 2001. Unfortunately there are no photographs of the worst Linton floods recorded before 1968, which were in August 1879 and April 1918.

In June 1968 more than 2.7 inches of rain fell in 24 hours leading to catastrophic floods in Linton. The rain was non-stop from 1pm on the Sunday and houses began to flood in the early hours of Monday morning. By Monday lunchtime the fire brigade had pumped out most of the floodwater. Locals blamed the floods on the barrier effect of the newly-constructed bypass.

The flood in October 2001, although not as severe as the one in 1968, nevertheless swamped the High Street as far as North's bakery shop and inundated all the properties close to the Swan Bridge and Meadow Lane.

Above. The 1968 Linton Flood. Some parts of the Grip were under eight feet of water and many properties had to be evacuated. This photograph of Hadstock Road with the railway bridge in the background shows serious flooding.

Below. The 1968 Linton Flood. This photograph resolves the argument about which flood was worse – the floodwater in 1968 was clearly higher than in 2001, almost reaching Market Lane close to the International Stores.

Above. *The 2001 Linton Flood, which extended up the High Street as far as North's bakery shop. It affected homes near Swan Bridge and Meadow Lane but the scale of damage to houses in the lanes off the High Street was less than in 1968.*

Below. *The 2001 Linton Flood. Firemen rescued residents trapped in their homes in Meadow Lane. The Dog and Duck pub is on the right. The area on the left was always known as Pond Close.*

Above. *The 2001 Linton Flood. Water damaged all the properties along the High Street as far as Paintin's offices. You can see the depth of the water in this photograph, but in 1968 the waters were at least a foot higher.*

Below. *The 2001 Linton Flood. The Church and Church Cottage had some damage but not on the scale of 1968. The Guildhall was built before 1527 and must have suffered a great deal from flood waters over the centuries.*

Above. One afternoon in early May 1913 a massive hailstorm hit the Cambridge region causing extensive damage to Bull House in the High Street, smashing 134 panes of glass in the Workhouse and flooding the High Street. A crowd gathered at the end of Balsham Road to gawp at the road surface which had been completely covered by melting hailstones.

Right. The great hurricane of October 1987 caused considerable damage in the village. A collapsing tree brought down the high brick garden wall of Linton House exposing to view the Wren-style mansion built by John Lone in 1698. The wall was rebuilt in 1989 at a cost of around £60,000.

Fire

Many local villages and towns have been destroyed or severely damaged by fire. Haverhill and Sawston have rich histories but very few old buildings survive; Linton however has survived virtually intact. Big fires in 1709 and 1829 were contained even though the fire appliances were primitive. For many years the second-hand 1911 engine, shown below, supplemented the old Napoleonic one and both went for scrap in 1940. In the 20th century, control of the fire service passed from the parish and district councils to the National Fire Service. Local Linton fire crews are shown here with their appliances.

Above. Linton Fire Brigade's Napoleonic fire engine on the recreation ground in 1906. Joe Gimson in the centre was the chief fire officer.

Left. At virtually every celebration held in the village, such as the Coronation in 1911 shown here, the fire engine was put on display. This replacement for the old Napoleonic one cost £40 in 1911. The engine was horse-drawn and manned by a crew of 12.

Below. A demonstration on the recreation ground in 1942 of the newly acquired Beresford Stork two-man trailer pump, supplied to the parish by the National Fire Service. Its duties included dealing with fires caused by incendiary bombs. Harold Mascall is on the left of the appliance and Vic Wilson behind it.

Above. Linton Fire Brigade in 1955 after the opening of the new fire station. The QL ex-army water truck, used from 1948 to 1955, was ideal for local fire fighting since it had four-wheel drive, could tow a trailer pump and carried more than 500 gallons of water. Harold Mascall was the chief officer (front row, second from the left).

Below. Linton Fire Brigade in the early 1960s, after the station had won the county efficiency award. From left to right in this photograph: Dave Mackay, Robert Pipe, Jack Ramsey, Neville Blake, Alf Tofts, Fred Fitch, Denny Chapman, Jim Vale and Harold Mascall. Harold retired as chief officer in 1977.

Above. Fire at the corner of Balsham Road on 10th May 1909. Flames engulfed the blacksmith's premises of William Norden and destroyed two thatched cottages causing £200 worth of damage. Water was 100 yards away and women rallied to organise a bucket chain while the men just watched and criticised.

Below. Fire at the Greenhill on 15th August 1910. Around 1.45pm a spark from a passing traction engine set fire to the thatched roofs of two cottages next to the Greenhill pub. The old Napoleonic fire engine ran out of water and by 5pm the two cottages were gutted. The owner Henry Prior, pictured below, built a new house on this site in 1911 and called it Phoenix House.

Water

The village was dependent on wells for its water supply until the construction of the water tower on Rivey Hill in 1936. The main public wells were located opposite the Swan Hotel near the present-day bus shelter, by the market place close to 32 High Street, at the top of Mill Lane and opposite the Tandoori restaurant near the house called the Anchorage. Only the one in Mill Lane survives.

Due to chronic water shortages in the 1920s and 30s, a new scheme for water supply was developed whereby a pumping station on Hildersham Road pumped water first to a water tower tank on Rivey Hill, and from there to local villages. This reliable water supply transformed life in the village. For example, it enabled a new central school to be built to cater for post 11-year-old pupils throughout the district – the Village College was born.

Above. *A water cart en route from Linton to local villages in 1933 during a period of severe water shortage, prior to the construction of the water tower.*

Below right. *The completed water tower in 1936. The tower itself cost £3788 and was part of a larger SCRDC scheme costing £46,000 which involved 10 local villages and more than 34 miles of pipework. During its construction a guard had to patrol each night to prevent locals climbing the internal staircase.*

Below left. *The Linton water tower nearing completion in 1935–6. Paintin's of Linton built the 33-metre brick tower which had a storage capacity of 87,500 gallons. Castle Camps was the first village to receive piped water in September 1936.*

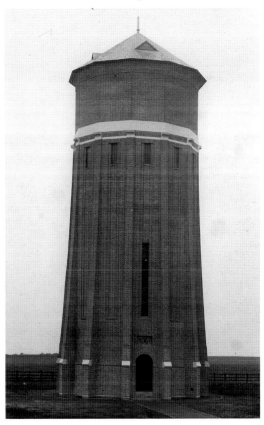

Shops and Businesses

Opposite. Linton Post Office in 1903. The sub-postmistress, Mrs Mary Moore, ran the business until her ill health forced closure in 1920. The post for most local villages was distributed from Linton and there were two deliveries daily until 1917.

Above. Linton Chalk Pit in 1959, the site of the Hadstock Road Industrial Estate today. The site was run by Linton Chalk and Whiting Company from 1919–41 and Lime Supplies of St Albans from 1947 until the late 1960s. Oswald Griffiths is on the centre tractor.

From 1281 the market in Market Lane had a near monopoly of local trade. Stalls and small shops were grouped by trades and this remained the situation until the early 18th century. The market then moved across the High Street to the Market Hall in the area now cobbled close to the former Literary Institute building. The 19th century witnessed a sharp decline in what had once been Cambridgeshire's third largest market, and Linton market finally closed in 1864. By that time the village teemed with shops of every kind and such an old-fashioned market had outgrown its usefulness.

Linton was a market town for the local area and had a thriving carrier trade to London and Cambridge long before the railway reached the village in 1865. The following pages show photographs of the main village shops arranged in order, starting in the Grip and proceeding along the High Street to Bartlow Road. Readers should recognise the locations since the High Street in particular has largely kept its 19th-century appearance. People had to shop daily when there were no domestic fridges or freezers so there was always a place for a small shopkeeper to open a business in a room of his or her house. Many of the shops were quite small, and the men of the household often worked in full-time employment, using the shop to supplement their income.

By the late 19th century the only large-scale industry in the village was the granary storage and milling business of Linton Mill in Mill Lane. In the 20th century the Chalk Pits in the Hadstock Road were developed on a larger commercial scale but ceased to operate by the early 1960s. Linton then attracted a new source of employment and for 20 years or more Cathodeon Crystals was the dominant employer in the village.

Linton still had numerous shops and small businesses until the early 1970s. Most have now disappeared but in the High Street you can still see many of the former shop fronts which had been added to much older houses in the trading boom of the 19th century.

Above. Coote and Warren coal merchants owned sidings at Linton railway station and operated in Linton from around 1900 to the 1960s, competition coming from Myhills of Walden. John Linsdell is on the left in this 1920s photograph.

Below. Herbert Powell's bakery around 1903, occupying the site where Greenhill Mews are today. The shop was extended around 1913 after the White Hart pub was demolished and the low flat-roofed shop later became the Greenhill Café. The bakery closed in 1944.

Above. No. 13 High Street was once the sweet and grocery shop of Mr George and this photograph, taken in 1939, shows from left to right: Eric George, Charlie Tofts, a Hills girl, Jack Tofts, Joyce Giles, Jim Norton and Joyce George. The shop closed in the 1960s.

Left. Tom Street and his daughter Barbara in the 1930s outside his fishmonger's shop at 15 High Street, close to the present-day Crown Inn. He was the first person in Linton to sell sausage and chips. He had been the landlord of the Greenhill pub before he bought the shop in 1933 for £250. It closed after 1945.

Above. *Taken around 1898 – the pavements had recently been laid and a gang of Tarmac workmen are standing in front of William Willis's hairdressing shop at 15 High Street. Mr Willis, who was also the local photographer, ran this shop from 1882 until 1922. The man holding the bucket is Mrs Toft's grandfather.*

Below. *The chemist's shop of EG Titmarsh at 29 High Street in 1968. The shop first became a chemist's in 1864 when Samuel Suckling moved here from Haverhill. Mr Coulthard and Mr Prain ran the business between the two wars. In the 18th century there was an inn on this site called the New Unicorn.*

Holttum's Store

The Holttum family ran a drapery and grocery store in the High Street at the end of Market Lane from 1855 when Richard Holttum came to Linton as a shop tenant from King's Lynn. He purchased the premises in 1876 and later added the Victorian extension on the left of the building to house the drapery section. To the left of that a further single-story extension was built in 1925. As sub-postmaster, he also ran the Linton post office in his main shop from 1869–1896.

In 1945 the shop, then run by Thomas Rule and Ernest Bullmann, was sold to International Stores who ran it until 1986. Gateway briefly ran a grocery business here until 1987 when it closed because the store was too small to compete with supermarkets and too expensive to refurbish.

Right. *The International Stores in 1985, two years before it closed.*

Below right. *Close up view of Richard Holttum senior's shop in 1900.*

Below left. *Staff standing at the main entrance to the shop in the early 1890s. The left part of the building is the Victorian drapery extension, and to the left of that is the garden wall with a gate that led to extensive storage sheds.*

A Shop Boy's Life

Gilbert Mills came from Willingham and was 15 years old when he went to work as an apprentice for a three-year period at Holttum's shop in Linton. The wages were 2/6d (12p) a year, but all his food and lodging costs were met. He had nine months' training before he was allowed even to serve customers. He wore a white coat and apron, worked from 7am until 7pm for five and a half days a week, lived in the attic area above the shop and had ten days unpaid holiday a year. He stayed at the shop for 20 years.

Right. The saddlers' shop of William and Mary Maris around 1910. They travelled around the farms in the district and had more than 40 local farmers on their books. The family business started here at 45 High Street in the 1830s and had closed by the 1950s.

Below. Beryl Burgess in the 1950s seen serving in James Bertie Sneezum's bakery, on the site of today's North's bakery. During the war the village siren was fixed in the shop's yard and Bertie was the chief ARP warden.

Above. Linton Post Office in 1990, next to Paintin's yard. Once the site of the saddling business of the Maris family, it became the post office under Mr Morton in 1962, then Mr Corker from 1964 and John Redding in 1984–91. The post office moved to its present location in 1992.

Below. HJ Paintin's workforce around 1928. Paintin's yard at 43 High Street has been used by builders since the 18th century. The firm built, among many other things, the Linton water tower and 42 houses in Balsham Road between 1927 and 1933.

Above. Nellie Butt's newsagent's shop in 1903, at the present-day 49 High Street, was first opened by Amos Butt in the 1840s. Their newsboys delivered the Cambridge Chronicle and the Independent Press.

Below. An 1895 view of 47 High Street, site of the the present-day electrical shop, which was then a hairdressing shop also owned by Nellie Butt, and later by Walter Seeley. Note the poor state of the road surface.

Right. The 18th century Market Hall seen here in 1910 was demolished in 1953. Shops and stalls once encircled this hall when the Linton market moved here from Market Lane in the early 18th century. The market finally closed in 1864. The hall once housed the cage, or prison, the village stocks and the Napoleonic fire engine.

Left. An 1880s photograph of the butcher's shop of Joseph Smoothy on the corner of Horn Lane, later the site of Barclay's Bank. There had been a butcher's shop and slaughter house on this site since 1798, and this old Tudor building was demolished in 1900.

Below. Len Culling was the butcher here from 1935 to the 1950s. Maurice Wright is on the left of the picture and Len Culling and his son are on the right. Mr Culling slaughtered two oxen, eight sheep and six pigs here each week.

Above left. *The Signal Box railway shop in the early 1980s owned by Alan Lawley; it is now Sweet Talk News. The business became one of the largest rail stockists in the region between 1979 and 1983.*

Below. *Len and Amy Colvill in 1975 shortly before the shop closed. Len took on the London Stores from his father and said that the shop, which specialised in groceries, haberdashery and knitting wools, "sold everything from a pin to an elephant".*

Above right. *A 1930s photograph of the London Stores in the High Street opposite the end of Coles Lane with the owners, Albert and Mary Colvill, pictured in the doorway and Bert Colvill by the window. The store opened in 1931 and closed in 1975. The owners, who ran the shop from 1931 to 1975, made their own lollipops, and their soda fountain was said to be the talk of the district.*

Left. Mrs Arthur Coxall with her children Stanley, Violet, Muriel and Lala, outside her hairdressing, newsagent's, fruit and vegetable shop on the corner of Church Lane around 1905. She ran the business from 1904 until the 1940s and her husband was the last licensee of the adjacent Axe and Saw pub, which closed in 1921.

Below. Alfred Forsdike's butcher's shop at 74 High Street around 1910. He was in business here from 1892 until 1930 and the old shop window can still be seen. Frank Hargrave was the butcher here in the 1930s, the Faireys in the 40s and 50s and the Nordens until the late 1960s.

Shops and Businesses

Right. The Carter family of Haverhill was in business at 80 High Street for almost 100 years until the 1950s. Initially there were two shops: one was a fancy repository, tobacconist and confectionery shop; the other a jewellers and watchmakers. Fire hooks were displayed here in 1913 for a visiting group of antiquarians led by William Palmer, the local doctor.

Below. An early 1920s photograph of Edgar Morley's post office, photography and newsagent's shop at 115 High Street. He bought the shop around 1910 and photographed most Linton social events for more than 50 years. He ran the post office here until 1961.

Above. In September 1912 military manoeuvres took place in East Anglia. The main clash between the two mock armies took place at Horseheath. Soldiers were stationed at Little Linton and Edgar Morley sold hundreds of papers to the troops, the Daily Mirror to the ranks and the Daily Telegraph to the officers. The latter paper issued the newsboys with boaters.

Below. The Mill and Mill House at Linton in 1910. A mill was first recorded on this site in 1222 and the buildings in the photograph date from the 18th century. By the 1850s the old water mill was equipped with a powerful beam engine. The Gowlett family owned the mill from 1908 until it closed in 1983 and was converted into houses.

Above. *This 1912 photograph shows Holttum's store on the left and the Co-op store on the right. Sarah Holttum, who ran the shop, came to Linton in the 1880s and Richard Holttum senior, her father-in-law, set her up with her own shop. She named the house after her home town of Bedford.*

Below. *The Co-op in 1908. Sawston Co-op opened their first branch in Linton in 1904. The shop was quite small then and sold Wheatsheaf branded products. The brick-built premises erected in 1887 were called Jubilee House to commemorate the 50 years of Queen Victoria's reign.*

Above right. *Photographed around 1910. John Collier ran a shoemaker's shop at 139 High Street from 1879 to 1929 in premises now owned by the Urwin family, the local vets. Many villagers can remember the large pear tree growing on the gable end wall.*

Above left. *During the inter-war period Stanley Coxall's fruit and vegetable shop was located opposite the Waggon and Horses pub. The shop was part of a row of cottages set back from the street known as Tudd or Townshend's Alley. Here you can see his Eldorado ice cream cart. All the properties were demolished by 1938.*

Left. *John Maris the manager of Holttum's branch shop standing in the doorway of the grocery business, then owned by the International Stores. Grocers and drapers had traded here from the early 19th century.*

Above. *A photograph taken around 1900 showing the blacksmith's shop of the Redhouse family at Clifton House near the start of Bartlow Road. The business operated from the 1880s until around 1930. Their business sign, a waggon wheel, can be seen near the group of children in the centre of the photograph.*

Below. *The offices of the Cathodeon Crystals factory in 1983, five years before it closed. The firm first opened a small factory in 1953 in Shepherds Hall, Market Lane, and by 1960 had moved to what is now the Copperfields estate. In the 1960s more than 400 people were employed here making silicon semi-conductor crystals for the rapidly growing electronics market.*

Above. *The cycle shop and wheelwright's business of the Rush family located opposite the end of Balsham Road. No. 132 High Street was a cycle shop from around 1904 until the 1930s, selling most makes of bicycle including their own Rush brand. To the left you can see the wheelwright's sheds.*

Below. *A photograph taken around 1922 of Albert Norton's fruit and vegetable shop in a wooden shed on rented farmland opposite his council house in Back Road. His son Bill is standing on top of the cart which was used to deliver their produce to local villages. The shop closed around 1930.*

Public Houses and Inns

Opposite. *The Waggon and Horses pub around 1900, owned by Henry Prior junior, the Grip brewer. It first became a pub in 1838 when Henry Prior senior bought the site for £300 from the Linton Poor Law Guardians, and the buildings facing the street became the new pub. On the left the 1737 Task House can be seen, where the village poor were set to work.*

Above. *An 1878 view of the White Hart Inn at the top of the High Street when Hawkes Brewery of Bishop's Stortford bought the premises for £398. It had been an inn since the 18th century but had declined in importance by the 1890s. Cars found it difficult to turn into the High Street and in 1911 the County Council bought the inn for £225 and demolished it to widen the road.*

Almost everyone seems to be convinced that every other house in Linton was at one time some kind of hostelry. Although this is not true, there were large numbers of drinking establishments in the village, especially in the 19th and early 20th centuries. Included here are photographs of the best-known establishments and as many of the lesser-known ones as space allows.

From the 16th century there were two large inns, later coaching inns, located in the central market area close to Market Lane. The Griffin, later called the Crown Inn, where local magistrates met and coaches stopped en route to London, operated until 1844–5. The Unicorn, later Red Lion, on the corner of Horn Lane was the largest inn and the centre of village social functions, as well as being a posting station for the Cambridge to Colchester stage coach.

In the 18th century two grand inns opened in the High Street just below the market area. The Bull and Chequer Inns were up-market meeting places for the gentry and closed later in the same century. The trade arising from the wagon route to Saffron Walden led to the opening of the Greenhill and White Hart public houses at the top of the High Street in the early part of the 18th century.

On the Bartlow side of the river the Swan Inn flourished from the early 17th century based on its location near the ford over the river Granta. The Bell Inn and the Old Dolphin, once standing near the Granta Vale site, were 17th-century establishments relying on the custom of tenants living in the Barham manorial area of the village. For a brief period in the 18th century the Marlborough Inn opened at what is now 100 High Street.

Employers usually provided beer for their employees as part of their wages. After the Beer Act of 1830, beer drinking increased because anyone could operate a beer house from their home for a low annual licence fee of £2 a year. Drunkenness became the curse of the Victorian age and new pubs and beer houses sprang up all over the village. Henry Prior, the local brewer in the Grip, opened the Waggon and Horses in 1838 and the Dog and Duck in 1850–1. At the top end of the High Street the Crown Inn, the Three Tuns brewery next door, the Racehorse public house and the George and Dragon beer house were opened. Beer houses served the poorest labourers with beer, but public houses were more up-market and could also offer spirits. At the other end of the village, the Tally Ho BH, the Princess of Wales PH, the Green Lane Malting, the Coach and Horses PH, the New Dolphin PH and the Wheatsheaf BH appeared. Most vanished by the 1920s but the Princess of Wales survived until recent times.

Of the three hostelries remaining today the Waggon and Horses has been open the longest.

Above. The Greenhill pub in 1918 shortly after Greene King bought out Christmas Breweries. There had been a pub on this site since 1728 and this was the most profitable of the local pubs owned by Henry Prior, the Grip-based brewer. It closed in 1997.

Left. View looking up the Grip towards Cambridge Road in 1898. Note how narrow the road was between the White Hart and the Greenhill pubs. Located by the street lamp on the left was Henry Prior's 19th-century Linton Brewery. He sold out to Christmas Breweries of Haverhill and the brewery closed around 1908.

Above. The Crown Inn
after a fire in 1907. Until
1845 the Crown coaching
inn was located at 35 High
Street and when it closed,
the former licensee opened
the present Crown Inn
on this new site. Phillips
of Royston bought the
property in 1899, and
today it is privately owned.

Right. The former Red
Lion coaching inn taken
around 1900. The inn was
known as the Unicorn until
1685 and coaches from
Cambridge to Colchester
stopped here, but they
ceased to operate when
the railway reached
Cambridge in 1845. In
1825 the Red Lion inn
fetched £1500 at auction
but when it closed in 1852
it barely made £250.

Above. Photograph of the High Street in the 1860s. The Old Crown coaching inn, formerly known as the Griffin, was first recorded in 1575. The gateway of the inn is next to the small girl on the right of the photograph, although by the early 18th century the building to the left of the gateway had become a grocery and drapery shop, which at this time was owned by Richard Holttum. The inn had closed by 1845.

Below. Pre-1867 photograph of the old wooden footbridge with the Dog and Duck beyond it. The names given to the bridge have changed over time: Barton's Bridge in 1600, Linton Bridge in 1680 and the present-day Swan Bridge after 1867 when it was built for £717. The Swan Commercial Inn on the right was first referred to as the Swan in 1616.

Above. There were 12 pubs in Linton in 1900 and still eight in 1939. The Dog and Duck was a working-class pub and only served beer. It first became a pub in 1851 and beer was supplied by Mr Prior's Brewery in the Grip. The photograph is dated 1900 when the landlord was Mr Day.

Below left. The Dog and Duck in 1919 after it had been renovated by the new owners, Greene King. Before 1851 the 16th-century cottages were owned by leather makers and butchers.

Below right. Bull House in 1913, once the 18th-century Bull or Black Bull Inn. The owners from 1700 to 1772 were the Linton lords of the manor and the inn was a meeting place for rich gentlemen of the village. Cock fights were held in the garden to the rear of the inn.

Above. The Swan Hotel in the 1880s. Hawkes of Stortford bought the Swan in 1878 for £965, and it was Linton's premier inn from that time until the 1970s. Cyclists and commercial travellers were its main clientele, and carriers to Cambridge used the yard at the rear. Note the roof line of the Swan and the state of the road surface.

Right. The Axe and Saw pub sign can be seen in this 1914 view down Church Lane. It was a down-market beer house which opened in the 1880s and was later bought by Tredway and Percy who sold it in 1919 for £530. A fire in the pub outbuildings in 1920 focused the attention of the sanitary authorities on the inadequacy of the drainage. It finally closed in 1921.

Left. The Bell Inn on the left and Tally Ho beer house on the right, both with signs outside, around 1870. Note the appalling state of the road surface. The Bell was owned by Boreham's of Burton End before 1881. The exterior was at this time covered in unsightly plaster and in 1918 it was removed to expose the wooden beams (see below and page 14). The Tally Ho at 78 High Street was a beer house catering for labourers which opened in the 1860s and closed by the 1890s.

Right. The Bell Inn around 1920. The first reference made to the 'Sign of the Bell' was in 1670 when it was owned by John Goodey. Greene King purchased the 49 pubs of Christmas Breweries in 1918 and spent £1694 on renovating the Bell. The beautiful old timbers were exposed then, once the plaster was stripped off.

Above. *1920s view of the Princess of Wales which had been a pub since 1838. In 1864 the licensee was blamed by the local school head teacher "for enticing a boy named Fuller Chapman to drink there". The boy was flogged in front of the whole school! Paintin's built a new pub of the same name on this site in 1936, and it finally closed in 1991.*

Below. *Ram House on the left, now 100 High Street, dates back to the early 17th century. In the 1720s the house was called the Marlborough Inn after the famous Duke who vanquished the French army at the battle of Blenheim in 1704. The Marlborough name was still used in 1793 even though the inn had long closed.*

Left. The former Maltings building in Green Lane in 1900 at the rear of 96 High Street. Robert and John Adcock operated their malting business in the 19th century and it rivalled Henry Prior's malting in the Grip. It closed in the late 19th century and the buildings were then used by Linton Laundry. Parts of the old malting buildings still survive.

Right. Horseheath Road and Bartlow Road junction before 1914. Two pubs can be seen in Bartlow Road: on the left is the Coach and Horses, in a building now called the Anchorage, and on the right is the Dolphin which closed in the mid 1950s.

Below. The Waggon and Horses pub in 1918 after its renovation by Greene King, with the old Task House to the left.

Schools

Infant School

The present Linton Infant School was originally the only school in the village, and catered for children from five right up to the school-leaving age of 14.

The earliest Linton school, recorded in 1558, was located inside the boundaries of the present-day churchyard close to the pathway from the Infant School. However, it was not until 1840 that Linton had a school that catered for the masses. The Rev Charles Keene was the lord of the Great and Little Linton manors and he provided the land for a National School controlled by the Church of England on the site of the present-day Infant School. This mixed school charged for attendance and did not become a free establishment until 1891. Children aged 5–12 went to this elementary school and the first headmaster was Mr Mutimer who was

Above. Class II of the infants in 1910. Miss Fleet, head of the infant department, is on the left and Miss Meeks on the right.

Opposite. From around 1907 most Cambridgeshire schools celebrated Empire Day (24th May) as seen in this 1909 photograph taken in the Linton Mixed School playground. Children saluted the flag, sang 'The Flag of Britain' and were given a half-day holiday. Arthur Samuels, the head teacher from 1902, is on the right.

there from 1840 until 1885. An infant section was added in 1875. The main school building was then extended in 1894 to cater for the influx of the free school pupils.

This arrangement continued until 1937 when the new Village College took the older pupils. Later still in 1974, in response to a growing population, Linton Heights Junior School was opened to cater for the 7–11 age group, under its new head teacher Bernard Reid.

Above. *In 1840 the Rev Charles Keene founded the Linton National Church of England School, which was an all-age mixed school for 5–12 year olds. The 80 fee-paying pupils were taught in the central part of the buildings; the left-hand section was added in 1864 and the right-hand section in 1894.*

Below. *This 1909 photograph of the 'babies' department shows Miss Fleet, on the left, who was head of the infants from 1909 until 1914. Note the clothing, the boy-girl seating pattern, the desks and chairs, and the very few pictures on the walls.*

School near to closure

A report by Her Majesty's Inspector, following his visit in April 1925, highlighted the poor condition of the school buildings and led to a demand for immediate repairs or closure. Linton children were educated in rooms with peeling paintwork, poor lighting, inadequate ventilation and minimal heating; the pail toilets often overflowed and there were no facilities for washing or drinking. Average class size was 46 in classrooms designed for 34 at most.

Above. *Linton infant class in 1930. Second from the left in the back row is Ray Noakes, second from the left in the middle row is Claude Perry and seventh from the left in the front row is Ivy Tofts.*

Right. *The school staff in 1912 with Arthur Samuels, head from 1902 until 1934, in the middle. Miss Fleet, the infant head from 1909–14, is third from the left in the front row.*

Below. *Miss Gwen Samuels with her infant class II in 1962. She was the daughter of Arthur Samuels, the former head teacher, and kindly donated a range of old photographs to the Historical Society.*

Above. *Miss Irene Morley's class at Linton Junior School in 1961. The 7–11 year olds moved to a separate school in 1974 when Linton Heights Junior School was opened. Note the former vicarage in the background.*

Below. *The Junior School football team in 1934–5 taken outside the main buildings of the present-day Infant School. Mr Woods, the new head teacher, was very keen on sporting activities. Note the variety in the footballers' kit.*

Village College

After the Great War the expense of providing an elementary education to the age of 14 proved too much for many village schools. They were unable to teach woodwork, cookery and physical education lessons (except drill) because of the costs involved. These inadequacies helped Henry Morris, the modern equivalent of the chief education officer for Cambridgeshire, to promote the revolutionary idea of a village college system.

In September 1937, Linton Village College opened with 308 children, and Mr Tomlinson was the first warden. It was the third such college to open in the county and children from 11 to 14 no longer attended their own village schools. After the Second World War the college became a secondary modern school, and in September 1974 it became a comprehensive for pupils aged 11 to 16, with John Heywood as the new warden.

Below. The design of the new classrooms was quite revolutionary. Educationalists enthused about the benefits of fresh air, plenty of light and flexible fixtures. Hence the sliding metal doors and huge areas of glass. Only girls did needlework and their first task was to make aprons for the boys' woodwork classes!

Above. The start of a new era in secondary education. The splendid new buildings by architect Mr S Unwin cost £21,000 in 1937.

Left. The fountain enhanced the approach to the beautiful front entrance of the new school, but proved too expensive to maintain and ceased to operate in 1950 after the college could not raise the £500 repair cost.

Below. A physical training class for boys in the college hall in 1940. The catchment junior schools had few facilities for games and this was one of the reasons why Henry Morris wanted Cambridge 11 year olds to attend specially built schools. Classes for sport were single sex.

Above. *1944–7 class photograph taken at the front of the Village College. Terry Moore and Sheila Norton are first and second from the left on the back row. School numbers were only 280 and the school leaving age was 14 until 1947. Edwin Swannell was the warden (head of the school and adult education) from 1939–64.*

Below. *The Village College football team in 1947–8 with their PE teacher, Jack Warren, who taught there from 1938–56. Note the original LVC badge. The temporary building provided when the school leaving age was raised to 15 in 1947 is in the background, and is still there in 2006!*

Above. *1950s photograph of the Village College. Note the single drive, the unspoilt approach to the entrance and the lovely gardens. Beyond the college on the right are Stanton's Lane, the Linton Hospital and Rivey Hill.*

Below. *Early 1960s photograph of Speech Day at the Village College. Mr Edwin Swannell (the warden) is addressing the parents and children; the chairman of the managers, Mr S Taylor, is next to the warden.*

Right. *Rosalie Swannell, the second warden's wife, is on the right of this 1945 photograph. The promotion of community education was a prime motive for building the village colleges. Over 250 adults enrolled in each of the three terms in 1937–8 and around two-thirds of them came from Linton.*

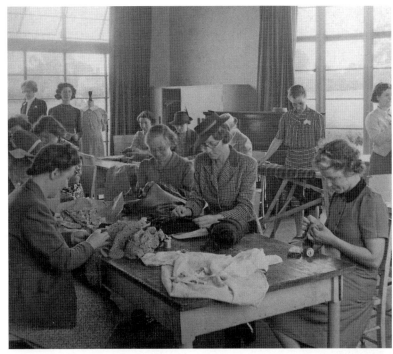

Below. *Linton Village College golden jubilee photograph in 1987. Mrs R Swannell was the guest of honour, and some of the first intake of pupils in September 1937 are in this photograph. Joyce Sneezum is in the centre of the front row and Jim Vale is on the extreme left of the back row.*

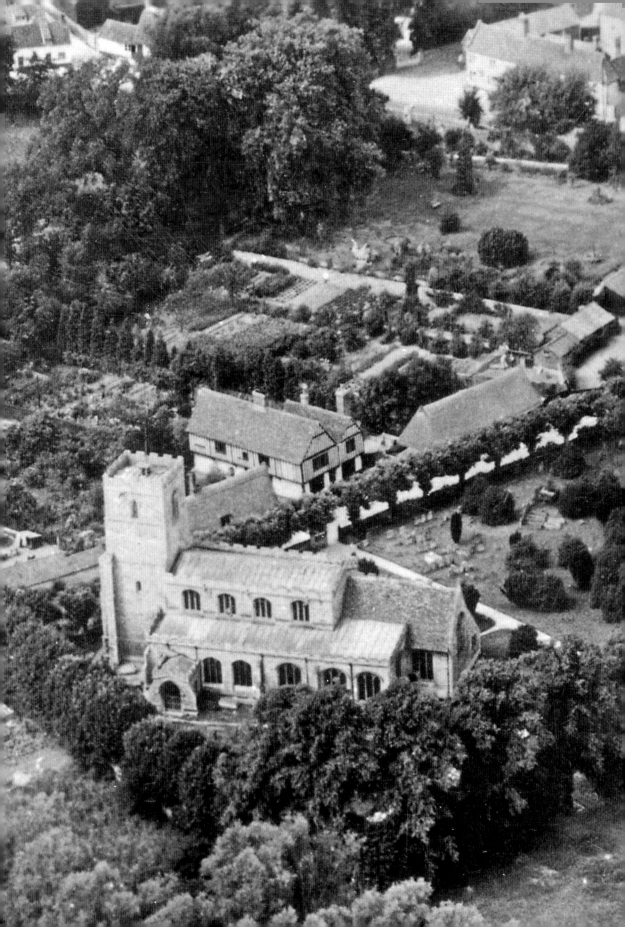

Church, Chapel and Guildhall

The first recorded mention of a church in Linton was in 1163 in correspondence between Pope Alexander III and the abbey of St Jacut de L'Isle in Brittany. The abbey owned Linton Rectory until it passed to Pembroke College in 1440.

There are still a few traces of the 11th-century Norman church, but most of the structure dates from the 14th and 15th centuries. The interior was restored between 1870 and 1880 when the old wooden pews were replaced by chairs. There are some excellent examples of monumental tombs in the church and two are quite outstanding. The 17th-century Millicent memorial, now hidden by the Victorian organ, symbolises the power of the Millicent lords of Barham. In the south aisle the marble Sclater-Bacon memorial displays the great wealth of the Linton lords who used to live at Catley Park.

__Opposite.__ A 1929 aerial view of St Mary's. The outward style of the building is largely perpendicular dating from the 15th century. Close to the church tower is the Guildhall.

__Below.__ The church in 1803 when the Rev Edmund Fisher junior was the vicar. The small bell tower had replaced the original spire which collapsed during the great storm of 1703.

Above left. *The church in 1853 was by this time in a very poor state of repair, the tracery in the windows was broken and many windows were bricked up. The doubling of the population between 1800 and 1850 led to serious overcrowding at services, made worse by the half-empty pews of the wealthier churchgoers.*

Below. *The church interior in the 1890s showing the new oil lamps. The building was completely restored between 1870 and 1880, ancient pews were replaced by chairs and the two galleries were removed. The east window dates from 1893 and cost £190.*

Above right. *A photograph from the mid 1890s shortly before the bell tower was removed. The ivy on the tower caught fire in August 1904 when a cyclist discarded a match after lighting his pipe, but prompt action by the verger saved the day. Choral services at the top of the tower on Ascension Day had to be abandoned that year because of drunken behaviour by youngsters in the congregation.*

Vicarages

Linton vicarage, located on the site of 117 High Street, was first recorded in 1280 when Geoffrey was appointed vicar by the bishops of Ely. In 1473, the vicar, Thomas Green, moved the vicarage to its present location near the river. However, the vicarage there proved too small and damp so later vicars tended to reside in grander Linton houses until 3 Church Lane was purchased in 1896. It remained as the vicarage until the present one was built in 1965.

Above. *The Old Vicarage in 1959 when a lorry coming from Linton Mill lost its steering and crashed into the 17th century building. An earlier building on this site was the home of Linton's first vicar in 1280 and two centuries later, in 1473, the site was given to Pembroke College in exchange for that of the present rectory.*

Below. *No. 3 Church Lane in 1900, which had become the vicarage house in 1896 when the Rev John Longe moved in with his new bride. The house had once been an up-market school.*

Above right. The Tithe Barn in the grounds of the Guildhall around 1912 shortly before it was demolished. As rectors of Linton, Pembroke College were entitled to the great tithe levied on corn. After 1841 the tithe was collected in cash so the now-redundant barn soon deteriorated.

Guildhall

The beautiful Guildhall was built between 1520 and 1527 and was the property of the Guild of the Holy Trinity. King Edward VI suppressed the guilds in 1547 but the building survived because the land on which it was built was owned by Pembroke College who were the rectors of Linton. A tithe barn in the grounds of the Guildhall was used to store 10 per cent of the grain crop which was given annually to the rectors as a tax called the great tithe.

Above left. The Guildhall around 1900. Built on Pembroke College land by the Guild of the Holy Trinity between 1520 and 1527 and used as a town house for entertainments and weddings by the village from 1564 until 1696. It then became the farmhouse of the 100-acre rectory farm leased out to tenant farmers by Pembroke College.

Below. The Guildhall in 1913, just after Pembroke College sold the building to Mrs Berney Ficklin for £600. She turned it back into a house and removed the wall plaster, exposing the beautiful beams and windows.

Left. In this photograph from 1900 the Guildhall and part of a 16th-century barn can be seen on the right. The Whiffin family, who were carriers, lived in the 16th century Church cottage for much of the 1800s. The ford by Horn Lane bridge was in constant use until the early 20th century.

Below. Linton church choir in the mid 1890s with the vicar, Rev John Longe, on the back row. The choir thrived under his leadership and were rewarded for their work by excursions to the seaside and Christmas treats at local big houses such as Horseheath Lodge.

Right. The wedding in 1919 at Linton church of 32 year old John Ross to Annie Morrell, 24. They are pictured here after the service in the school playground and George Morrell, sitting by the driver, was the youngest child and only son in a family of nine children. Annie's father was foreman at Myhill's granary, opposite the present-day Village College.

Below. The Church Lads Brigade of the 1st St Mary's Company in December 1919 in the vicarage garden at 3 Church Lane. The Rev Rutter established the brigade in 1906 and Rev Ernest Edwards revived it shortly after the end of the Great War when 18 boys, who had to be churchgoers, joined up.

Church Lads at 'War'

Fourteen teenagers from the Linton Church Lads Brigade under the command of Lieutenant Bowen set out by train for Shelford on Easter Monday 1907 for a field day. They marched from there with the Cambridge Company to the Gog Magog Hills and stormed the wood at the top which was defended by the Shelford brigade. The umpire, Captain Touch, judged that the assailants had carried the position and they all marched back to Shelford for a hearty tea, arriving home in Linton by 7.30pm.

Below. The Church Lads Brigade outside the Linton Mixed School around 1906. Boys aged 13–18 were trained and drilled on military lines. They had been issued with new belts, caps and haversacks and after six months' training were allowed to drill with rifles, which were kept in the school.

Chapel

The first dissenter chapel in Horn Lane faced the river side rather than the lane itself and was finished in 1698. A new chapel was constructed in 1818 and most of the £1000 cost was met by the Taylor family, who were wealthy tanners residing in Green Lane. The Sunday School hall was built later, in 1908, on part of the Manse garden.

Below. An 1890 photograph of the Congregational Chapel in Horn Lane, which was built in 1818 at a cost of £1000. The original chapel was constructed in 1698 beside what was then a smelly tannery on the Springfield house site. The grand tombs reflect the wealth of the shopkeepers and traders who formed the backbone of the non-conformist church.

Below. The opening ceremony of the Congregational Sunday School hall and lecture room in Horn Lane in September 1908. The Sunday School was founded in 1799 and its 150 members needed a larger meeting place. Miss Hailes of Linton made the whole project possible by donating £300 to the building fund.

Social Gatherings

Opposite. Linton Hospital Sunday Parade around 1925. These parades were the traditional way to raise money for Addenbrooke's Hospital and most local villages had similar functions. The marchers represented all the local village organisations and assembled at the Greenhill to march to the recreation ground for tea and sporting events.

Above. Linton Salvation Army band around 1930. The Salvationists came to Linton in 1886 and bought the present-day Amy Hall in the High Street in 1919.

Below. Young men of Linton looking cool and dressed to impress in this pre-1914 photograph, possibly taken near Chilford Hall. Charlie Moss is in the middle and Mr Creek on the left.

Above. *A 1925 photograph of Linton Wolf Cubs in which the two boys at the back are holding the Cambridgeshire Wolf Cub banner and totem pole. Mr Whiffin on the left was in charge of the Linton pack and they had just won the Wolf Cub Football Challenge Cup, held here by Jim Tofts, beating Shelford cubs 3–0.*

Below. *The river near the mill in the present-day Pocket Park contained deep pools in the area locals called the Island. Boys and men used the fishermen's bridge to dive into the water which was up to 10 feet deep. Take a good look at the local male talent in the late 1920s!*

Above. Every old Lintonian remembers Dr Palmer's wild flower shows which were held for the schoolchildren in his large garden at Richmonds in Symonds Lane. The Doctor is on the left by the trees.

Below. Linton Guides in the early 1920s. Miss Mercia Purkis, the leader, is in the centre of this photograph taken in the vicarage garden at 3 Church Lane. In January 1921 they entertained 60 elderly people in the Infant School and carried lanterns to see them all safely home.

Above. *Linton Granta Football Club's 50th anniversary in 1951 held at the Village College. A club had been formed on two previous occasions before Tom Chalk firmly established it in 1901. They played in the Thursday Cambridge and District League and their ground was off Back Road in the Rivey Way area.*

Below. *The Linton British Legion in the early 1920s in front of the old Market Hall in the High Street, which was pulled down in 1953. Linton had formed a branch of the Comrades of the Great War in 1919 when 108 local men joined. The name had changed to the British Legion by the time this photograph was taken.*

Above. *A May 1949 visit to the Palace of Westminster by the members of the fourth year of Linton Village College. Mr R Jones was in charge of the group and they met the local MP Mr AE Stubbs. He had been elected for Labour in 1945 and was the first Labour member to be elected in our constituency.*

Below. *Linton Granta Football Club in 1937–8. The club was tremendously successful in the 1930s and swept all before them. In this season they won the Haverhill and District League, the Russell Cup and the Cambridgeshire FA Premier League. Tom Chalk, the founder of the club in 1901, is sitting by the trophy on the left.*

Farming

Until the Second World War, farming was the major employer in the area, taking about two-thirds of male school-leavers.

Great and Little Linton manor farms remained largely intact until recent times. The Keene family owned the Linton estates from 1772 until 1904, and the Wilkin family retained control until the 1950s. Their main farmlands were to the west of the water tower and stretched as far as Hildersham, the Roman Road and Hadstock. The main farms were tenanted and included Little Linton, Catley Park, Chilford Hall and the Grip.

Lands to the east of the water tower are now owned by both Pembroke College and the Fairey family. The college inherited the Great and Little Barham estates from Mrs Sarah Lonsdale in 1807 and these stretch as far as the Roman Road, West Wickham Road by Horseheath Lodge and Bartlow village. The main farms were tenanted and included Great and Little Barham, Heath Farm, Emsons, Finchams, Greenditch and the Wheatsheaf farms.

Smaller farmsteads were located nearer the village and photographs of some of these are included in this chapter.

There is a shortage of local photographs on this subject. Perhaps readers will be able to help with photographs from their own collections.

Above. 1920s farming scene on the Little Linton Farm of Sam Taylor when the horse was still dominant and muscle power made up for the lack of farm machinery.

Opposite. Livermore's farm just off the High Street opposite the Co-op in the 1920s. There was a small farm here in the 18th century called Zenkers, named after the Quaker family of John Zincke, and during the inter-war period Harry Wright kept a few dairy cows and delivered milk.

Below. Small homesteads were very common in the pre-1939 farming scene; they were usually rented and located close to the village. Albert Norton rented land in the 1920s by the chalk pit in Back Road and is pictured with his horse and plough close to his council house.

Above. *Little Linton Farm around 1916–18. There was an acute labour shortage in the latter stages of the Great War and female workers of the newly-formed Land Army were drafted in to work on our farms to replace the men who had been called up.*

Below. *Little Joiners Farm in Market Lane around 1910. A fire in 1949 destroyed the 300 year old thatched cottages, leaving the 1651 chimney as the only original feature. Roughly 35 acres of land was attached to the farm; part of the holding included the present-day Dovehouse Close site.*

Above. Forestry was very important in this area, timber sales providing up to a quarter of farmers' incomes. This 1912 photograph taken in Borley Wood, owned by Pembroke College, includes members of the Perry family, who were lath renderers and hurdle makers.

Below right. Little Linton Mill in 1900, six years before it ceased to operate. There had been a mill here in 1086, located downstream from Little Linton manor. The manorial lords of Great and Little Linton operated the mill as part of their farmland estate.

Above and below left. On 16th June 1904 two steam engines were ploughing on Catley Park Farm (shown above, demolished in 1978) on the slopes above Camgrain. A steam gauge on one engine failed to warn of overheating and at 6pm the engine blew up. A piece of flying metal struck and killed 21 year old Frederick Mynott who lived in the cottage in the background.

Linton at War

The two world wars had a major impact on every community in Britain and Linton was no exception. The 1912 army manoeuvres in East Anglia involved the first large-scale use of aerial reconnaissance in warfare and the final battle at Horseheath produced the kind of military stalemate later experienced on the Western Front. The visit of King George V was an unexpected bonus.

While local volunteers and regulars went off to the front or joined the navy, the war had an immediate impact on villagers with the arrival of Belgian refugees and wounded soldiers. Many were housed in Symonds Lane workhouse and later at Manor House in Coles Lane.

Excitement and curiosity gripped the village in 1917–18 with the arrival of around 100 German prisoners of war at the workhouse and their regular forays into the village to work on local farms were eagerly awaited by local children. When the war ended in November 1918, joy was muted by the large numbers of returning wounded soldiers and the loss of 47 Linton men, but a celebratory mood was more apparent in 1919 after the Versailles peace settlement had been signed. In 1920 a German field gun was placed by Swan Bridge on a raised plinth as a symbol of the allied victory (see photograph on page 13). Our local war memorial was unveiled in Linton cemetery in 1921.

***Opposite.** 1944 photograph of a parade by local groups for Salute the Soldier Week. The Linton Home Guard are seen here marching by Myrtle Cottages, which were opposite the Crown Inn and have since been demolished. Lieutenant John Collier was the officer in charge of the Linton platoon of the 3rd Cambridgeshire Battalion.*

***Below.** In September 1912 there were widespread army military manoeuvres in our region. Thousands of soldiers camped in the present-day Village College catchment area. King George V is shown at Little Linton talking to Crimean War veteran Robert Linsdell. This photograph appeared on the front page of the Daily Mirror.*

Above. Linton and district volunteers could sign up in Linton, Cambridge or Bury St Edmunds and the first eight local volunteers for Kitchener's Army are pictured here at Linton station in August 1914. On the left of the front row is George William Cracknell.

Above and right. Belgian soldiers recuperating in the autumn of 1914 at the Linton Red Cross VAD Hospital in the Linton workhouse, Symonds Lane, consisting of two wards for about 24 soldiers. This hospital closed in June 1915 and patients moved to the Manor House (right) located at the corner of Coles Lane and the High Street. Upstairs there were five wards and a surgery, and the men had to walk to the workhouse for baths since the facilities at the Manor House were inadequate. The hospital closed in 1919 and the house was demolished in 1939.

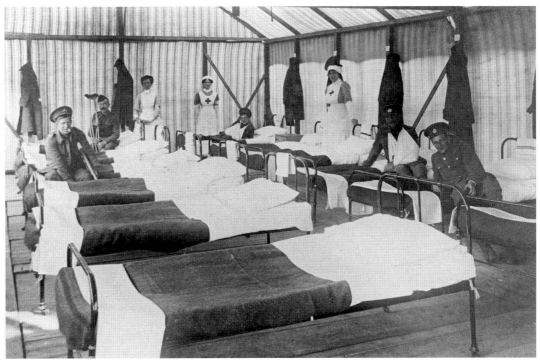

Above. The hospital at the Manor House had 39 beds, and 14 men were placed in tents in the garden, which ran the length of Coles Lane. Hospital staff cared for 648 British and 32 Belgian wounded during the course of the war.

Below. Dr Palmer pictured around 1917 in the grounds of the Manor House with 25 nurses and two guiders. Mrs Edith Smith of Chilford Hall Farm was in charge of the hospital, which also had 15 male nurses.

Above. In May 1917 the guardians of the workhouse in Symonds Lane converted the hospital wards and the main yard into a prisoner of war camp for 100 German prisoners who were assigned to work on local farms. This photograph shows local soldiers preparing the camp.

Below. Soldiers on duty in 1917 near Linton workhouse, Symonds Lane, where around 40 men guarded prisoners of war. By July 1917 there were more than 100 prisoners, working eight hours a day on local farms. Two German soldiers died there and were buried in Linton cemetery.

Above. National Peace Day was celebrated all over the country on 19th July 1919 to celebrate the signing of the Versailles treaty. This photograph shows the Linton parade assembling at the Greenhill before marching to the cricket meadow for a children's tea party and sports.

Below. Linton War Memorial was unveiled on 13th March 1921. The memorial was erected to commemorate the sacrifice made by the 47 Linton men who lost their lives during the Great War.

Second World War

The 1939–45 war involved fewer local casualties than the First World War, but affected the civilian population much more because of the large number of airfields in our region and consequent attacks by German aircraft. Troops were stationed at Chilford Hall, Queen's House, Shepherds Hall, Horn Lane, Catley Park, Little Linton and Bartlow. Tanks were seen in the streets in the early years of the war and were based at varying times in Joiners Road, the Grip, Bartlow Hall and Abington.

The Village College was the main centre for the billeting of evacuees and provided a canteen for local voluntary organisations. The headquarters of the ARP was at Bertie Sneezum's bakery in the High Street, where the village siren was also located and gas masks were fitted and checked out. The Home Guard HQ was in Shepherds Hall and later transferred to the Old Market Hall. The Red Cross and WVS were very active and used The Beeches in Green Lane, the Red Cross hut in Coles Lane and the Village College for their essential wartime work. Linton fire service, which scrapped its old fire engines in 1940, was initially based in Market Hall and then moved to Symonds Lane. The Observer Corps had an observation post in Hollow Lane and did stalwart service in spotting and tracking enemy aircraft. Ration books were issued from the Literary Institute building but also sometimes from private homes.

Cadet groups for boys and girls were based at the Village College. Scouts and Guides contributed to the war service by escorting evacuees to their billets and by making house-to-house collections for salvage, especially paper and cardboard.

The village supported and housed constant influxes of evacuees, and the names of many of them are recorded in school registers, although the attendance registers for 1939–41 have unfortunately been lost. Celebrations and parades continued throughout the war years.

Left. *1944 photograph of a parade by local groups for Salute the Soldier Week. Shown here are the Linton detachment of the Red Cross, and Linton Guides led by Miss Nunn.*

Below. *The Cambridgeshire Battalion pictured in Market Lane, 1939–40, as they were about to leave for camp at Brandon. Jim Norton is fourth from the right on the front row and on the far right of the middle row is Maurice Wright who died in the Far East, as did many of the Cambridgeshires.*

Above. Army manoeuvres using tanks were a regular event in our region during the early part of the war when a German invasion of East Anglia seemed a real possibility. The photograph was taken in 1939 near 101 High Street.

Below. Tanks were stationed in Linton at various times during the war and were based in Joiners Road, the Grip and Coles Lane. This photograph was taken at the top of the High Street between 1939 and 1941.

Left. *Linton Air Cadets in 1942–3. The 1451 Flight of the Air Training Corps Haverhill Squadron, run by Flight Lieutenants Williams and King, was based at Linton Village College and boys aged 14–18 were eligible to join.*

Below. *The 3rd County London Yeomanry were billeted at Chilford Hall in 1940–1. Rowley and Hayden Smith, the tenant farmers, used to transport them into Linton on their tractors and trailers.*

Right. *Members of the Linton Observer Corps in 1940 manning the observation post at their base in Hollow Lane, opposite the Village College, where parts of the structure can still be seen. Many of the local trade and professional classes joined the corps; Arthur Samuels is on the right.*

Above. *The officers of the Cambridgeshire Home Guard. The local commanding officer, Colonel Foster of Hildersham, is seated in the middle of the front row and the officer in the back row (marked with a cross) is Lieutenant John Collier, the commander of the Linton platoon of the 3rd Cambridgeshire Battalion.*

Below. *On VE Day in May 1945 there was a church service and parade by all the wartime organisations. Tea was organised for the village children in Green Lane and tables were decorated with red, white and blue crepe flowers.*

Acknowledgements

I have received a great deal of help over the years from a wide variety of people and organisations. I am especially indebted to the Cambridgeshire Collection and the Antiquarian Society for allowing me to use an extensive range of photographs from their archives. Chris Jakes and his team have been extremely helpful.

For the text used with the photographs I am indebted to Mr R Stevens who has kindly given me access to materials from his extensive research into Linton history; to Iris and the late Frank Jeffery for their work on Linton housing; to the late George Seaman-Turner and Peter Taylor for their loans of photographs in the early years of my research; to the County Records Office; to Pembroke College, Cambridge, and their archivist Jane Ringrose; to Ian Stratford for permission to use his Hawkes & Co. pub photos of 1878; to Julian's Photography for permission to use their photos of the 2001 floods; and to Aerofilms for allowing me to use their 1929 aerial view of Linton. The source of individual photographs are acknowledged below.

My sincere thanks are extended to the numerous local people whom I have interviewed and who have been kind enough to let me copy photographs of their family or of Linton. I am immensely grateful to the members of the Historical Society committee, in particular to Pat Genochio, Alex Todd, Frank Appleyard and Andrew Westwood-Bate for their support.

Finally I want to thank the Linton News and Norman Dann for all the sound advice and help they gave me in the preparation of this book. Without Norman's expertise in scanning photographs and arranging the page layouts I would not have been able to produce this book. I would also like to thank Alan Judge, Gloria Fidler and Kate France for proofreading, and Sally Simmons for her professional advice and final edit. Of course any factual errors are mine and I am always grateful if members of the public point out my mistakes so that I can correct them later.

The free distribution of this book to all readers of The Linton News has been made possible by a generous grant from Local Heritage Initiative, a partnership between the Heritage Lottery Fund and Nationwide Building Society.

Garth Collard

Picture Credits

While every effort has been made to trace and obtain permission from copyright holders, the author would be pleased to have any errors or omissions brought to his attention. The photographs are reproduced in this book by the kind permission of the Cambridgeshire Collection and the Antiquarian Society unless specifically listed below:

Aerofilms, 9, 84; Norman Allison, 45br; Barbara Birch, 32m, 102, 108t; Lewis Burden, 66b, 62t; Mrs D Byatt, 93b, rear cover; Diane Coe, 56tr, 56b; Garth Collard, 6, 19t, 29b, 32b, 36, 37b, 38t, 38b, 41b, 51tr, 51br, 53t, 62b, 76t, 83b, 101m; Mr G Collier, 109t, 111t; Mr D Cottage, 94b; Don Coxall, 61tl; Mr & Mrs J Cracknell, 42t, 104t; Ray Dobson, 111b; Gary Hall, 33tl; Alan Hardy, 5; Mrs M Griffiths, 47; Sheila Hatfield, 31tr, 63b, 99b; Julian's Photography of Linton, 39t, 39b, 40t, 40b; Alan Lawley, 56tl; John Linsdell, 48t, 99t; the late John Maris, 52t, 61b; Harold Mascall, 43b, 43t; the late Irene Morley, 78b, 78t; Morley family, 33tr; Jack Noakes, 93t; Jack Noakes and Ivy Tofts, 77t; Dr Naughton, 35b; Jim Norton, 49t, 107t; Mona Rumsey, 34t, 107b, 109b; the late Gwen Samuels, 74, 77m, 77b, 89b, 105b; Joyce Sneezum, 52b; Ian Stratford, 65; the late Edwin Swannell, 79t, 80b, 81b; Ivy Tofts, 50t, 95t; Ian Trotter, 35tl; David and Val Urwin, 61tr; Barbara Walker, 49b; Andrew Westwood-Bate, 42b; Jane Wheatley, 101br.